Francis Frith's
AROUND LINCOLN

PHOTOGRAPHIC MEMORIES

Francis Frith's
AROUND LINCOLN

◆

Martin Andrew

FRITH
BOOK Co

First published in the United Kingdom in 2000 by
Frith Book Company Ltd

Hardback Edition
ISBN 1-85937-111-6

Paperback Edition 2001
ISBN 1-85937-380-1

British Library Cataloguing in Publication Data

Francis Frith's Around Lincoln
Martin Andrew

Frith Book Company Ltd
Frith's Barn, Teffont,
Salisbury, Wiltshire SP3 5QP
Tel: +44 (0) 1722 716 376
Email: info@francisfrith.co.uk
www.francisfrith.co.uk

Printed and bound in Great Britain

Contents

◆

FRANCIS FRITH: *Victorian Pioneer*

FRANCIS FRITH, Victorian founder of the world-famous photographic archive, was a complex and multitudinous man. A devout Quaker and a highly successful Victorian businessman, he was both philosophic by nature and pioneering in outlook.

By 1855 Francis Frith had already established a wholesale grocery business in Liverpool, and sold it for the astonishing sum of £200,000, which is the equivalent today of over £15,000,000. Now a multi-millionaire, he was able to indulge his passion for travel. As a child he had pored over travel books written by early explorers, and his fancy and imagination had been stirred by family holidays to the sublime mountain regions of Wales and Scotland. 'What a land of spirit-stirring and enriching scenes and places!' he had written. He was to return to these scenes of grandeur in later years to 'recapture the thousands of vivid and tender memories', but with a different purpose. Now in his thirties, and captivated by the new science of photography, Frith set out on a series of pioneering journeys to the Nile regions that occupied him from 1856 until 1860.

INTRIGUE AND ADVENTURE

He took with him on his travels a specially-designed wicker carriage that acted as both dark-room and sleeping chamber. These far-flung journeys were packed with intrigue and adventure. In his life story, written when he was sixty-three, Frith tells of being held captive by bandits, and of fighting 'an awful midnight battle to the very point of surrender with a deadly pack of hungry, wild dogs'. Sporting flowing Arab costume, Frith arrived at Akaba by camel seventy years before Lawrence, where he encountered 'desert princes and rival sheikhs, blazing with jewel-hilted swords'.

During these extraordinary adventures he was assiduously exploring the desert regions bordering the Nile and patiently recording the antiquities and peoples with his camera. He was the first photographer to venture beyond the sixth cataract. Africa was still the mysterious 'Dark Continent', and Stanley and Livingstone's historic meeting was a decade into the future. The conditions for picture taking confound belief. He laboured for hours in his wicker dark-room in the sweltering heat of the desert, while the volatile chemicals fizzed dangerously in their trays. Often he was forced to work in remote tombs and caves

where conditions were cooler. Back in London he exhibited his photographs and was 'rapturously cheered' by members of the Royal Society. His reputation as a photographer was made overnight. An eminent modern historian has likened their impact on the population of the time to that on our own generation of the first photographs taken on the surface of the moon.

VENTURE OF A LIFE-TIME

Characteristically, Frith quickly spotted the opportunity to create a new business as a specialist publisher of photographs. He lived in an era of immense and sometimes violent change. For the poor in the early part of Victoria's reign work was a drudge and the hours long, and people had precious little free time to enjoy themselves.

Most had no transport other than a cart or gig at their disposal, and had not travelled far beyond the boundaries of their own town or village. However, by the 1870s, the railways had threaded their way across the country, and Bank Holidays and half-day Saturdays had been made obligatory by Act of Parliament. All of a sudden the ordinary working man and his family were able to enjoy days out and see a little more of the world.

With characteristic business acumen, Francis Frith foresaw that these new tourists would enjoy having souvenirs to commemorate their days out. In 1860 he married Mary Ann Rosling and set out with the intention of photographing every city, town and village in Britain. For the next thirty years he travelled the country by train and by pony and trap, producing fine photographs of seaside resorts and beauty spots that were keenly bought by millions of Victorians. These prints were painstakingly pasted into family albums and pored over during the dark nights of winter, rekindling precious memories of summer excursions.

THE RISE OF FRITH & CO

Frith's studio was soon supplying retail shops all over the country. To meet the demand he gathered about him a small team of photographers, and published the work of independent artist-photographers of the calibre of Roger Fenton and Francis Bedford. In order to gain some understanding of the scale of Frith's business one only has to look at the catalogue issued by Frith & Co in 1886: it runs to some 670

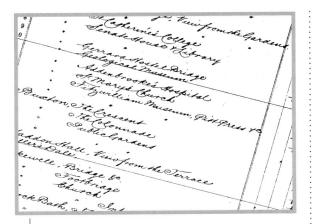

pages, listing not only many thousands of views of the British Isles but also many photographs of most European countries, and China, Japan, the USA and Canada – note the sample page shown above from the hand-written *Frith & Co* ledgers detailing pictures taken. By 1890 Frith had created the greatest specialist photographic publishing company in the world, with over 2,000 outlets – more than the combined number that Boots and WH Smith have today! The picture on the right shows the *Frith & Co* display board at Ingleton in the Yorkshire Dales. Beautifully constructed with mahogany frame and gilt inserts, it could display up to a dozen local scenes.

POSTCARD BONANZA

The ever-popular holiday postcard we know today took many years to develop. In 1870 the Post Office issued the first plain cards, with a pre-printed stamp on one face. In 1894 they allowed other publishers' cards to be sent through the mail with an attached adhesive halfpenny stamp. Demand grew rapidly, and in 1895 a new size of postcard was permitted called the court card, but there was little room for illustration. In 1899, a year after Frith's death, a new card measuring 5.5 x 3.5 inches became the standard format, but it was not until 1902 that the divided back came into being, with address and message on one face and a full-size illustration on the other. *Frith & Co* were in the vanguard of postcard development, and Frith's sons Eustace and Cyril continued their father's monumental task, expanding the number of views offered to the public and recording more and more places in Britain, as the coasts and countryside were opened up to mass travel.

Francis Frith died in 1898 at his villa in Cannes, his great project still growing. The archive he created continued in business for another seventy years. By 1970 it contained over a third of a million pictures of 7,000 cities, towns and villages. The massive photographic record Frith has left to us stands as a living monument to a special and very remarkable man.

Frith's Archive: *A Unique Legacy*

FRANCIS FRITH'S legacy to us today is of immense significance and value, for the magnificent archive of evocative photographs he created provides a unique record of change in 7,000 cities, towns and villages throughout Britain over a century and more. Frith and his fellow studio photographers revisited locations many times down the years to update their views, compiling for us an enthralling and colourful pageant of British life and character.

We tend to think of Frith's sepia views of Britain as nostalgic, for most of us use them to conjure up memories of places in our own lives with which we have family associations. It often makes us forget that to Francis Frith they were records of daily life as it was actually being lived in the cities, towns and villages of his day. The Victorian age was one of great and often bewildering change for ordinary people, and though the pictures evoke an impression of slower times, life was as busy and hectic as it is today.

We are fortunate that Frith was a photographer of the people, dedicated to recording the minutiae of everyday life. For it is this sheer wealth of visual data, the painstaking chronicle of changes in dress, transport, street layouts, buildings, housing, engineering and landscape that captivates us so much today. His remarkable images offer us a powerful link with the past and with the lives of our ancestors.

TODAY'S TECHNOLOGY

Computers have now made it possible for Frith's many thousands of images to be accessed almost instantly. In the Frith archive today, each photograph is carefully 'digitised' then stored on a CD Rom. Frith archivists can locate a single photograph amongst thousands within seconds. Views can be catalogued and sorted under a variety of categories of place and content to the immediate benefit of researchers. Inexpensive reference prints can be created for them at the touch of a mouse button, and a wide range of books and other printed materials assembled and published for a wider, more general readership - in the next twelve months over a hundred Frith local history titles will be published! The

See Frith at www. francisfrith.co.uk

day-to-day workings of the archive are very different from how they were in Francis Frith's time: imagine the herculean task of sorting through eleven tons of glass negatives as Frith had to do to locate a particular sequence of pictures! Yet the archive still prides itself on maintaining the same high standards of excellence laid down by Francis Frith, including the painstaking cataloguing and indexing of every view.

It is curious to reflect on how the internet now allows researchers in America and elsewhere greater instant access to the archive than Frith himself ever enjoyed. Many thousands of individual views can be called up on screen within seconds on one of the Frith internet sites, enabling people living continents away to revisit the streets of their ancestral home town, or view places in Britain where they have enjoyed holidays. Many overseas researchers welcome the chance to view special theme selections, such as transport, sports, costume and ancient monuments.

We are certain that Francis Frith would have heartily approved of these modern developments, for he himself was always working at the very limits of Victorian photographic technology.

THE VALUE OF THE ARCHIVE TODAY

Because of the benefits brought by the computer, Frith's images are increasingly studied by social historians, by researchers into genealogy and ancestory, by architects, town planners, and by teachers and schoolchildren involved in local history projects. In addition, the archive offers every one of us a unique opportunity to examine the places where we and our families have lived and worked down the years. Immensely successful in Frith's own era, the archive is now, a century and more on, entering a new phase of popularity.

THE PAST IN TUNE WITH THE FUTURE

Historians consider the Francis Frith Collection to be of prime national importance. It is the only archive of its kind remaining in private ownership and has been valued at a million pounds. However, this figure is now rapidly increasing as digital technology enables more and more people around the world to enjoy its benefits.

Francis Frith's archive is now housed in an historic timber barn in the beautiful village of Teffont in Wiltshire. Its founder would not recognize the archive office as it is today. In place of the many thousands of dusty boxes containing glass plate negatives and an all-pervading odour of photographic chemicals, there are now ranks of computer screens. He would be amazed to watch his images travelling round the world at unimaginable speeds through network and internet lines.

The archive's future is both bright and exciting. Francis Frith, with his unshakeable belief in making photographs available to the greatest number of people, would undoubtedly approve of what is being done today with his lifetime's work. His photographs, depicting our shared past, are now bringing pleasure and enlightenment to millions around the world a century and more after his death.

AROUND LINCOLN – *An Introduction*

Lincoln and the Cathedral:
'Never was an edifice more happily placed, overtopping a city built on the acclivity of a steep hill'.
(Robert Southey)

LINCOLN IS A city I have known virtually since birth, for my mother comes from Gainsborough, twenty miles to the north, and we spent many holidays there with my grandparents. My grandfather, Wilfred Durdey, had been joint managing director of Rose Brothers, the packaging machinery company after which Cadbury's named their Roses chocolates assortment. The factory was demolished in the 1960s to make way for Gainsborough's riverside gardens, and the town, claimed by many to be the location for George Eliot's 'Mill on the Floss', has greatly changed since the 1950s snapshot in the six views in this book.

My brother and I were often were taken as boys to Lincoln; I grew to love the great minster church and the older parts of the city, with coffee or tea in the Eastgate or the White Hart hotels as the simpler treats of a now distant age. Consequently, together with numerous visits over the years since, I have come to know the city and this part of Lincolnshire well and have a strong affection for it. Quite rightly: for it is a richly historic city with areas, uphill in particular, which have almost entirely escaped the rebuilding mania of the 1960s. Downhill (the city has two distinct areas) and mainly to the south of Stonebow there was a fair amount of injudicious new build, although the more recent new buildings have been more successful and less stridently intrusive. Certainly enough of the historic city remains to make a visit richly rewarding, quite apart from the cathedral minster church: this is of European importance in terms of medieval architectural history as well as being visually stunning and dominant.

Lincoln is situated on the limestone range of hills that runs roughly north-south in the western part of Lincolnshire. Although it is not high in alpine terms, and narrow, the ridge rises to over four hundred feet where it enters the county south of Grantham, and is two hundred feet high just south of Lincoln. The River Witham cuts across the ridge at Lincoln, and in so doing gave the site of the city great strategic significance. This part of Lincolnshire and north to the Humber is fairly flat, apart from the rolling chalk Wolds well to the east and Lincoln Cliff, as the limestone ridge is known, north of Lincoln. Consequently the minster's towers can be seen for miles, from as far away as Gringley on the Hill in Nottinghamshire over twenty miles away to the north-west, from the Boston Stump thirty miles to the south-east, and even from the North Sea, it is said.

However, the history of Lincoln starts long before the cathedral was even thought of, for it was the Roman invaders after 43 AD who recognised the strategic importance of the site. The Ninth Legion arrived here to cross the River Witham around 47 AD in the invaders' steady advance from the south coast. They found a marshy river valley with a large number of shallow pools to the west, two of which survive, Swan Pool and Brayford Pool. There was earlier settlement here, but the Romans gave the city its basic form. The Roman name 'Lindum' probably derives from the British and Welsh 'llyn' or lake; we can assume the area to the west and east of the immediate limestone ridge was marshy, for Roman works of drainage and control included cutting the Foss Dyke, both as a trade canal to link the town with the River Trent to the west and as part of this control regime. They canalised part of the River Till and turned Brayford Pool into a shipping basin, as well as canalising the River Witham as far as Bardney and cutting the Sincil Dyke. Of this work the Foss Dyke and Brayford Pool remain, although the Witham has subse-

quently been further canalised after the 1812 Witham Act.

Of just as great importance to the present town is the layout of the Roman one. The former Roman military road, later known as the Ermine Street, utilised the limestone ridge on its route from London to Lincoln and then, after 50 AD or so, northward to York, the subsequently as the basis of the Roman walled town of 41 acres; it became in 71 AD a 'colonia' or settlement for retired Roman legionaries. It thus acquired the name Lindum Colonia, subsequently in Anglo-Saxon times changing from 'Lindocolonia' to 'Lindcylene' to Lincoln.

The Roman north gate to the city, the

main Roman centre of northern Britannia. The Fosse Way, the military road that briefly formed the Roman frontier from Lincoln to Axminster in Devon, had its junction with Ermine Street near South Common, before Ermine Street crossed the Witham valley on a causeway along the course of the present St Catherine's and the High Street, then climbing steeply up The Strait and Steep Hill back onto the ridge. The legionary fortress occupied the area of the present castle and minster and immediately north. This was laid out Newport Arch, still stands to this day, while the lower parts of the East Gate have been excavated and are exposed in a pit alongside modern Eastgate. Parts of the wall and its course survive or have been excavated: its original southern line runs roughly along the castle south boundary and immediately south of Minster Yard. However, the city proved too successful, and grew downhill towards the river and the trading areas, so the walls were extended in the second century AD to enclose a further 56 acres as far as the line of

Newland, Guildhall Street and Saltergate, with the famous Stonebow the new south gate's successor.

The Roman walls formed the basis of the medieval walls, and of the division of the medieval city that succeeded the Roman. In effect, the upper town became the outer bailey to the Norman's castle, and was called The Bail, with the stretch of Ermine Street that bisects it called Bailgate, 'gate' being Danish for street. The lower enclosed area became the basis for the medieval city proper, together with medieval settlement east and west of the city walls and south along High Street through the older village of Wigford to the south. The Bail area had its own leet court until 1861 and came under the jurisdiction of the constable of the castle until 1835.

However, I have jumped too far ahead in the city's history, for after the Roman occupation ended Anglo-Saxon settlers and the older British occupied the city. Lincoln itself may have been the capital of the Anglian kingdom of Lindsey, whose royal genealogy is known, but which was absorbed by the kingdom of Mercia in the 7th century AD. Lindsey was converted to Christianity by Paulinus of York in 627 AD; a stone church was built which was probably the seat of the bishopric of Lindsey, although the church itself was burned down by Mercian raiders before the kingdom's conquest.

All was to change, for the Anglo-Saxon chronicle entry for 838 AD records that in Lindsey 'many men were slain by the host', the armies of Danish raiders who crossed the North Sea in their much-feared longboats. So successful were the Danes that the English had to cede all of England north-east of Watling Street to Danish rule in 886 AD. The whole area of Danish control was known as the Danelaw, with those areas in what is now Lincolnshire, Nottinghamshire, Leicestershire and Derbyshire being divided up among five of the Danish armies. These areas were heavily settled by Danes, and the area is now thick with Danish place names amid the Anglo-Saxon ones. The armies utilised the Roman road system for defence and each had their chief town or borough: two former Roman towns, Leicester, and Lincoln, and the towns of Derby, Nottingham and Stamford. However, English reconquest under King Edward the elder ended the Danish rule by 920 AD, but Lincolnshire retained Danish institutions and laws at least until after the Norman Conquest. Lincoln was by now a wealthy trading town and one of the most important in England, with a 1086 Domesday Book population estimated at around 7,000.

All was not peaceful for long. During the reign of Ethelred the Unready, Danish raiding and invasion led to Gainsborough being briefly the capital of a conquered England when Swein Forkbeard, King of Denmark, wintered there in 1013-14, indeed dying there in February 1014. In 1066 William, Duke of Normandy, invaded and defeated King Harold at the Battle of Hastings, and Lincoln was about to enter a new era under Norman rule. The Anglo-Saxon Chronicle records under 1068 that William the Conqueror built the castle, as well as those in York and Nottingham.

The Norman arrival certainly changed the town, for the older northern sector, the first Roman walled area, was appropriated by the conqueror for his castle, and the rest of this area became its outer bailey or forecourt. A third of the area within the walls was cleared, involving demolishing upwards of 166 houses, and the great castle was raised. There is much Norman stonework here surviving in the core of the present walls; a visit is a crucial part of touring the city. Throughout the Middle Ages the town walls were patched, rebuilt and repaired and ditches re-dug, which only disappeared gradually after Tudor times; the gates, medieval and Roman, were mostly demolished in the 18th century.

More visible, however, and from further away, is the next phase of the Norman city: the Cathedral. The seat of the Anglo-Saxon see of Dorchester on Thames was moved by William to Lincoln. Remigius, who had been bishop since 1067 in return for providing a ship and twenty knights for the invasion force, claimed control of Lindsey as well the rest of the huge bishopric that ran from the Thames to the Humber, a claim hotly disputed by the Archbishops of York. However, he moved north in 1072 and immediately started work on his new cathedral. It had a giant 'westwork' which survives as the lower part of the present west end. Its original design and purpose is still controversial: historians currently suggest that it may have been a fortified rectangular bishop's palace. Its three giant arched niches flanked by smaller ones survive, and it is certainly a most puzzling structure. Finished by 1092, the minster church east of the west block has been replaced. Remigius' west end was, however, retained and altered and surmounted by towers raised by the mighty Bishop Alexander after a fire in 1141. The rest of Alexander's work was swept away by the great Gothic church that followed. This rebuild was necessitated by a spectacular earthquake in 1185: from this tragedy one of

Europe's most important medieval cathedrals emerged, initially under St Hugh of Avalon, bishop from 1186 to 1200. His eastern transept and choir survive, but his east apse was replaced by the sublime Angel Choir, mainly to house his relics and to accommodate the flow of pilgrims following his canonisation. St Hugh's relics were translated amid great ceremony into the Angel Choir in 1280. The nave had been rebuilt by the 1230s, and the longer cathedral of St Hugh burst through the Roman east wall. This bald description of events does little justice to the wonderful, awe-inspiring qualities of the cathedral, which is surmounted by its three richly crocketted towers. These were once crowned by lead-clad timber spires which raised the central tower's height to an astonishing 530 feet, the highest in Europe. This blew down in 1548, but the western spires, lower of course, survived until 1807.

The cathedral close was also surrounded by walls, which were licenced by the king in 1285. Finished by 1327, some of the walls survive, along with two of the gateways: Exchequer Gate facing the castle, and Pottergate to the east (Priory Gate is a Victorian reconstruction). There are many superb and historic buildings within the close and throughout the upper town, and many in the lower town, not least the Stonebow medieval gateway and guildhall, and High Bridge carrying its timber-framed houses. However, the most remarkable survivals of the earlier medieval city are the Norman house, the Jew's House and, to the south, St Mary's Guildhall - these are rare 12th-century medieval secular stone buildings. Besides these, there are of course numerous later medieval buildings, many with timber-fram-

ing either exposed or concealed within later Georgian and Victorian brick casings. The descent from the castle and cathedral down Steep Hill and The Strait is truly memorable, and when you pass through Stonebow the immensely long High Street has more treasures to offer: Anglo-Saxon church towers, a Tudor water conduit, High Bridge and the Corn Exchange are but a few. The Brayford Pool area and Broadgate offer more rewards in a city whose historic areas can be walked around in a day as a taster, but you will be back again and again. Round a corner you will come upon an historic building tucked away, or upon a medieval remnant such as the old Greyfriars infirmary off Broadgate, now a museum.

The city suffered from some poor re-building in the 1960s and 1970s, and the road improvements have done Broadgate and Pelham few favours. The city fathers also allowed the warehousing around Brayford Pool to be swept away. But by and large later decisions were sounder, and the historic fabric of the city is in better heart than at any time I can recall. A book like this can only give a flavour of how the city has changed between about 1890 and 1960, but shows it also before the redevelopment mania of the twenty years after that turned Lincoln into its present appearance. Gainsborough, the other town in this selection, suffered far more loss; there was even talk of demolishing the uniquely important Old Hall to improve town centre car parking in the 1950s. We have moved on since then to a deeper appreciation of the value of historic buildings in establishing identity and in attracting the visitors such towns need to survive the near total loss of their heavy industry.

THE CITY FROM CANWICK HILL 1890 25622
Looking north past the chimneys of Hill Rest where the
B1188 climbs out of the valley cut by the River Witham
through the limestone ridge, this view shows how the
great Gothic minster cathedral dominates the city.
A few factory chimneys still survive in the Victorian
industrial south of the city in the middle distance.

BRAYFORD POOL 1890 25620
The Brayford Pool was the canal basin for the Roman
city at the end of the Foss Dyke canal, cut to link it
with the River Trent. This view shows it when it was
still a commercial inland port. Today the warehouses
on the left, now altered and rendered, are virtually the
sole survivors of this phase in its history.

THE CATHEDRAL FROM BRAYFORD POOL c1950 L49051

The Roman Foss Dyke canal fell out of use during Anglo-Saxon times, but was restored after the Norman Conquest to become one of the main outlets for the great medieval city's wool and lead exports. In 1950 there was still some trade, but it is now solely used by leisure craft and the warehouses on the right have gone.

THE CATHEDRAL FROM BRAYFORD c1965 L49227

The Witham flows from the south into Brayford Pool and out eastwards towards the North Sea under the foot-bridge, now replaced by a fly-over. Only the Royal William pub on the left, and a few cottages beyond, survive by the Pool; the warehouses on the right have now regrettably been replaced by offices and flats.

THE CATHEDRAL
from Pelham Bridge c1955

The area south-east of the city was marshy and virtually undeveloped until its draining after the Witham Act of 1812. It rapidly became the industrial heartland of the city along the now canalised Witham. This bleak view from the Pelham Bridge shows the influence of modern road improvement on a city landscape.

◆

BROADGATE c1955

Closer to the city centre, Broadgate is nowadays a frantically busy dual carriageway, and the site on the left a bus station. The spire of James Fowler's 1870s St Swithun's church behind the timber-framed Green Dragon pub orientate the modern viewer. Screened by St Swithun's is the 13th-century infirmary or hospital of medieval Greyfriars friary.

THE CATHEDRAL FROM PELHAM BRIDGE c1955 L49126

BROADGATE c1955 L49188

BROADGATE c1950 L49009

Here Broadgate starts to climb out of the valley. Whites Mineral Waters was rebuilt in 1994 as a county library, but the battlemented and towered former Drill Hall of 1890 survives. Beyond, at the corner of Silver Street, is the old constitutional Club of 1895, lots of blood red terra cotta, with the Usher Gallery beyond.

THE SCHOOL OF ART 1890 25663

Just off Broadgate, on Monks Road, is the former Lincoln School of Art, now the Gibney Building of the De Montfort University. The buildings to the right and the wall to the left have long been replaced, but the Dutch-influenced building of 1885 is seen here almost brand-new, with its elaborately scrolled gables and lead-clad tur-

THE CATHEDRAL 1890 25624
Lincoln's great minster church towers above the pantiled roofs. It is one of the finest cathedrals in England, and was begun by Remigius, who moved the see north from Dorchester on Thames to the old Roman town of Lincoln in 1072. The first Norman church was finished by 1092, but only the west part survives, now framed by Gothic work.

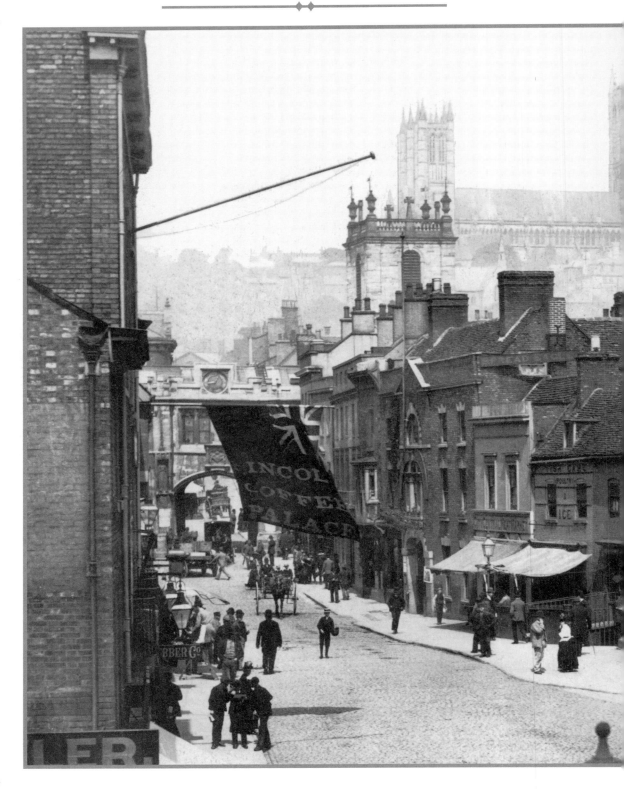

THE CATHEDRAL AND STONEBOW 1890 25654
This marvellously evocative late Victorian view from
south of High Bridge captures the character of the city
well. Many of the buildings that line the High Street
have been rebuilt, some of them twice since 1890, while
St Peter at Arches church, whose Georgian tower peers
over the rooftops, was demolished in 1933.

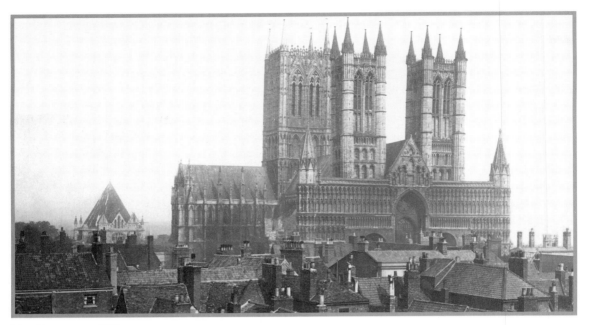

THE CATHEDRAL 1890 25625
The lower parts of the tall west towers are also Norman work, for Bishop Alexander substantially rebuilt the cathedral after a fire in 1141. Again, only the west part of this church survives, and what you see is mostly the rebuild started after a spectacular earthquake in 1185.

THE CATHEDRAL 1894 34835
The cathedral was once even grander, for it used to have lead-clad spires that took the height of the central tower from 271 feet to over 500 feet, the tallest in Europe and a beacon to shipping in the North Sea. The spire blew down in 1548, but the west tower spires survived in increasingly rickety condition until 1807.

THE CATHEDRAL 1895 35544

In this late Victorian view from in front of numbers 12 to 14 Minster Yard, the quality of the mainly 13th-century Gothic cathedral comes over well. The present Minster Yard roadway cut the old churchyard in two, but several of the slabs and tombs remain, albeit without the railings.

THE CATHEDRAL FROM THE SOUTH EAST 1900 46770

The transepts on the left were built for the energetic and inspirational bishop, St Hugh of Avalon, after the disastrous 1185 earthquake. He died in 1200 before the east end was finished, and the nave was not completed until the 1130s. St Hugh was canonised in 1220, and the east end was rebuilt by 1280 as the glorious Angel Choir to contain his relics.

THE CATHEDRAL, SOUTH PORCH 1895 35547
Known as the Judgement Porch from its carved scenes of the Last Judgement, it led into the Angel choir, the east arm
of the cathedral built for St Hugh's Shrine, and was probably used by pilgrims who would leave by the north porch
opposite. It was built about 1260 but is greatly renewed; a 1930s Virgin and Child now occupies the central niche.

THE CATHEDRAL 1890 25628

This view of the south side of the cathedral is taken from within the Vicars Court, where the vicars lived. Their function was to stand in for the normally absentee cathedral dignitaries and Prebendaries. The west range here, although mostly medieval, was much changed in 1875. Beyond is the Preceptory, with its dark-painted Georgian sash windows inserted into medieval stonework.

THE CATHEDRAL 1890 25629

This view from an upper window across Eastgate shows the north side of the minster with the back wall of the cloisters on the left. Started in about 1290, and dwarfed by the mighty transept and crossing tower, they were not strictly necessary in a non-monastic cathedral, but many medieval secular cathedrals acquired them, including Chichester and Salisbury.

THE CATHEDRAL, TENNYSON STATUE 1906 55109
Just outside the Close, beyond the cloisters and Chapter House, is this powerful statue of Lord Tennyson, one of Lincolnshire's greatest sons, born in Somersby on the Wolds. The statue, a bronze by George Frederick Watts, was erected in 1905; it shows the Poet Laureate contemplating some flowers with his dog at his side.

POTTERGATE AND THE CATHEDRAL 1890
The minster cathedral's medieval close
was once completely walled and entered
by six gatehouses. Of these, Exchequer
Gate, opposite the Castle, and Pottergate
survive. Priory Gate, near Eastgate road, is
a confection of 1816 built with old materials on the site of the medieval one. This
view shows the 14th-century Pottergate,
which was heavily restored in the 1880s.

POTTERGATE AND THE CATHEDRAL c1950
In 1938 the gatehouse was turned into a
traffic island when the wall at the right
in photograph No 25656 was demolished. The road now only takes foot traffic, and the 1950 bollards and road signs
already have a period flavour.

POTTERGATE AND THE CATHEDRAL 1890 25656

POTTERGATE AND THE CATHEDRAL c1950 L49054

MONKS ABBEY 1890 25667
This rural scene, about a mile east of the city centre along
Monks Road, is now much changed. This monastic cell of
St Mary's Abbey in York, of which the chancel remains, is
now in a municipal park and is surrounded by a bowling
green and fenced football pitch. The chancel of about
1300 is surrounded by railings.

THE CASTLE 1890 25668
This view of the Castle is from high on the west front of the Cathedral, looking past the Close's
14th-century Exchequer Gate. Parts of the walls surrounding the bailey are Norman. Building
the castle, which was started in 1068, involved the demolition of upwards of 160 houses.

THE CASTLE GATEWAY 1890 25670
The next two chapters can be followed as a walk which starts from the Castle and descends to the lower town. You enter the Castle from Castle Yard via the monumental east gate. The angle towers are 14th-century, but the stone tunnel vault you pass under is part of the original Norman late 11th-century phase.

THE CASTLE 1906 55111
Within the bailey is the Observatory Tower, where much restored medieval work is crowned by the 19th-century toy turret. It is on a mound, as is the Lucy Tower, which is in fact the late 12th-century keep.

THE CASTLE GATES c1955 L49106

This view looks back at the east gate from within the bailey. The inner drum towers are cheery early 19th-century, and something of a contrast to the outer side's rugged simplicity. Within the gateway is the re-set John of Gaunt's House oriel window, which was taken from a house in the town and a delightful 15th-century design.

THE CASTLE GROUNDS c1955 L49097

Opposite are the Assize Courts by Robert Smirke. Dating from 1823, they are in a pallid and unconvincing Gothick, its symmetry giving away the fact that Smirke was not designing in his normal Neo-Classical style. At the left is the corner of John Carr of York's Georgian County Gaol of 1787: no attempt here to match the castle's Gothic architecture.

CASTLE HILL 1906 55115A
This view looks from in front of Exchequer Gate towards the Castle. The buildings on the right are a splendid mix: the jettied timber-framed Tudor building of about 1543, with its three gables, contrasts with the early Georgian warm red brick houses beyond, and even more so with the austere and precise Judge's Lodgings of 1810 in pale stock brick.

CASTLE HILL AND THE CATHEDRAL c1965 L49232
Here we look from the Castle towards Exchequer Gate and the cathedral's monumental west front. The gabled timber-framed building had its render removed during restoration by the then National Provincial Bank in 1929. Given to the cathedral by the National Westminster Bank after a further restoration in 1970, it is now the tourist information centre.

BAILGATE c1955 L49112

BAILGATE c1955

Turning left out of Castle Hill, Bailgate follows the course of the Roman Ermine Street towards the old Roman north gate from the city, the Newport Arch. This was built in the 3rd century AD and is still partly standing, although it has had to be rebuilt several times when vehicles misjudged its height.

◆

EASTGATE c1955

This view is along Eastgate, east of the crossroads with Northgate ('gate' being Danish for street, rather than gate) and Minster Yard. Number 18, on the left, was refronted in the 1770s in brick with Venetian windows (with their centre part arched), and a later Greek Doric-style porch added.

EASTGATE c1955 L49108

STEEP HILL C1955 L49063

Retracing our steps to Castle Hill, we begin our descent to the High Street. Steep Hill is a very famous narrow and steep hill that has been much photographed over the years. This view looks uphill to the timber-framing and gables of Number 9 Castle Hill, now the Tourist Information Centre, which closes the vista admirably.

STEEP HILL c1965 L49201

This view looks down Steep Hill from nearer Castle Hill, with the jettied and timber-framed Spinning Wheel Restaurant on the far left, its later Georgian bow windows tucking under the jetty. The building on the right is now the Wig and Mitre pub. Steep Hill retains its stone flag footway and central roadway laid with stone setts.

STEEP HILL c1955 L49074

Further down we come to the crossroads with Michaelgate and Christ's Hospital Terrace. On the corner of Michaelgate is The Harlequin, again a good timber-framed and jettied building; it was formerly the Harlequin Inn and is now an antiquarian bookshop. On the left is a corner of the Norman House, built in stone around 1180.

STEEP HILL c1955 L49073

As we look past the Harlequin, the road steepens sharply past the junction with Danesgate by the railings. In the distance is the spire of St Swithun's Church off Broadgate, dating from the 1880s. Steep Hill now has a number of antique shops and antiquarian bookshops, which give you a chance to pause on your way down hill.

STEEP HILL c1955 L49034

Down past the Danesgate junction, we are in the most photographed section of Steep Hill - where it is truly steep. Syson and Sons, Furniture Dealers, has now been replaced by Readers Rest, an antiquarian and second hand bookshop which also occupies St Michael's Parish Hall of 1926 just out of view on the right.

STEEP HILL 1923 74640
This 1923 shot shows people toiling uphill past Syson's, with the timber-framed upper storey of Harding House Gallery on the right. This house was stone-built to the lower floors and timber-framed to the third storey, and has been much rebuilt. It is called Harding House because it was given to the City by a Canon Harding.

STEEP HILL C1950 L49035
The railings across the road at the Danesgate junction were said to have been installed to prevent a mad-cap Colonel driving his coach and four at breakneck speed down the hill! The view is now slightly touristified by the high wall on the right which has a notice board, including a map dispenser, set against it.

STEEP HILL 1906 55115

Although the big tree on the left has gone, the view is little changed. Number 10 retains its oriel bay windows but has had its brickwork painted white, while the house at the left, Number 9, is now a gifts and games shop, continuing in some form Mr Haigh's 1906 toy and fancy repository business.

STEEP HILL C1965 L49199

This view is taken slightly further down Steep Hill, just below the junction with Well Lane at the right. Just out of picture on the corner of Well Lane is one of the elegant water pumps installed by the City Corporation in the mid 19th century in a tapering cast-iron housing with the city coat of arms prominently displayed.

THE JEW'S HOUSE, STEEP HILL AND THE STRAIT c1955 L49055
The Jew's House is another of Lincoln's surviving early medieval stone houses: the city has more than most. It was a merchant's house with shops on the ground floor and the hall and chamber on the upper floor; the hall was heated by a stone fireplace above the doorway. To the left The Strait descends towards the High Street.

THE JEW'S HOUSE 1890 25664
Now the headquarters of the society for Lincolnshire History and Archaeology, the Jew's House dates from the 1170s and was indeed once owned by a Jewess, Belaset, in the 1280s. At the rear is Jew's Court, where, it is said, Little St Hugh of Lincoln was crucified by Jews in 1255: all utter nonsense of course.

THE STRAIT C1955 L49083
This view looks uphill from almost the bottom of The Strait towards the central tower of the cathedral. This section of the street has mostly late 18th- and early 19th-century brick fronts over the shops, some of which are now restaurants as well as antique shops.

HIGH STREET c1950 L49028
The gabled white building closing the vista north up the
High Street is now O'Neills pub, and is the first building
of The Strait. This section of the High Street had a lot of
inter-war rebuilding, including an Art Deco Burton's of
1933, now Edward's Coffee House, on the left,
and a Neo-Georgian Boots on the right.

SILVER STREET c1950 L49011

Lincoln suffered a lot of demolition in the 1950s and 1960s, including No 12 on the far left, now drab 1970s offices, and the buildings beyond which made way for the Stonebow Centre shopping mall of 1981. At the far right is a rather good Venetian Revival building of 1873.

SILVER STREET c1950 L49027

Almost all went on the right, in sequence: the Stonebow Centre, then a five storey office block replacing the tall Italianate building with urn finials, and then beyond is now the Silvergate Centre. More survives on the left: the former Courts department store, Neo-Georgian of 1922, and beyond the faience-fronted Pierre-Victoire.

STONEBOW c1950

This view looks towards the Stonebow from the High Street, with the former Courts store on the left still surviving. The shops on the right were replaced by awful 1960s buildings with coloured panels under the windows. In Silver Street, Battles, next to Stonebow, has also gone.

STONEBOW 1890

This wonderful atmospheric view looks through Stonebow into the continuation of High Street which follows the line of the Roman road to London, later known as Ermine Street. To the right is the grandiose Italianate bank of 1883 by the noted architect John Gibson, now the Natwest Bank; its fine banking hall has recently been very well restored.

STONEBOW c1950 L49010

STONEBOW 1890 25658

STONEBOW C1950 L49026
Through Stonebow you pass out of the area of the walled Roman and medieval city. The current gateway is later 15th-century - the left-hand and centre archways and the masonry above is least altered. Pearson added the battlements and extended the building in the 1880s, but the upper floor is basically Tudor and was the old city Guildhall.

THE GUILDHALL 1890 25657

We have now passed through Stonebow into the southern part of the High Street, which grew up along the old Roman road south of the walled city. The buildings visible through the main archway all went after World War I; then, prestige and chain stores such as Burtons and Lincoln's own department stores congregated in the area between Stonebow and The Strait.

STONEBOW 1901 46773

The Hepworths shop in photograph No 25657 was taken over by a local bank and given a splendidly bulbous and fruity Flemish-style ground floor soon after 1890. Indeed, in 1924 the bank liked the style so much it demolished the building on the far left and added a further bay in the same style. Later the Midland Bank, it is now the HSBC.

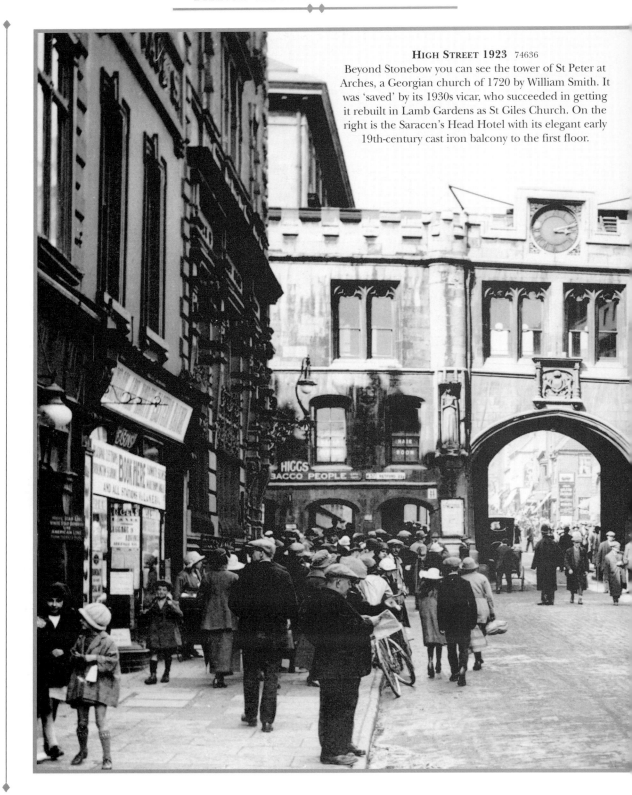

HIGH STREET 1923 74636
Beyond Stonebow you can see the tower of St Peter at Arches, a Georgian church of 1720 by William Smith. It was 'saved' by its 1930s vicar, who succeeded in getting it rebuilt in Lamb Gardens as St Giles Church. On the right is the Saracen's Head Hotel with its elegant early 19th-century cast iron balcony to the first floor.

STONEBOW C1955 L49115

This view of the Stonebow shows the length of the long open room on the top floor: this is the old city Guildhall, with a fine open timber roof of about 1520. At the right, on the roof, is the Mote Bell, one of the oldest in England, which has since 1371 rung to summon the city council to the Guildhall.

STONEBOW C1950 L49021

The buildings to the left of the bank have all gone, including the splendidly arched one, in 1950 the Regal Super Cinema, and the then up-to-the-minute shopfront of Kendall's; they have been replaced by a bland 1960s building for Littlewoods.

HIGH STREET C1950 L49053
In the niches either side of the central arch of Stonebow are statues of the Archangel Gabriel and the Virgin Mary, an Annunciation scene in effect. Over the central arch the royal arms of James I were added early in the 17th century, while the clock dates from the 1880s restoration.

STONEBOW C1955 L49120

The Saracens Head Hotel has gone the way of many smaller town centre hotels; it is now converted to shops and offices, including the bookshop Ottakars. The mock timber-framing of Woolworths, built in 1923, replaced some good Georgian town houses, and has now gone in its turn.

HIGH STREET C1965 L49215

The towering and somewhat two-dimensional timbered front of Woolworths and the 1907 Perpendicular Gothic-style Mac Fisheries (a chain long departed from our high streets) were recently demolished to make way for the High Street facade to the Waterside shopping centre, a large and successful 1990s scheme fronting Waterside North. The High Street is now pedestrianised.

HIGH STREET 1906 55114

We have now crossed High Bridge and are looking back along High Street towards Stonebow. The two Georgian buildings behind the obelisk were demolished shortly after this view was taken. Those beyond went in 1923 for the mock timber-framed monster of Woolworths, itself also now gone.

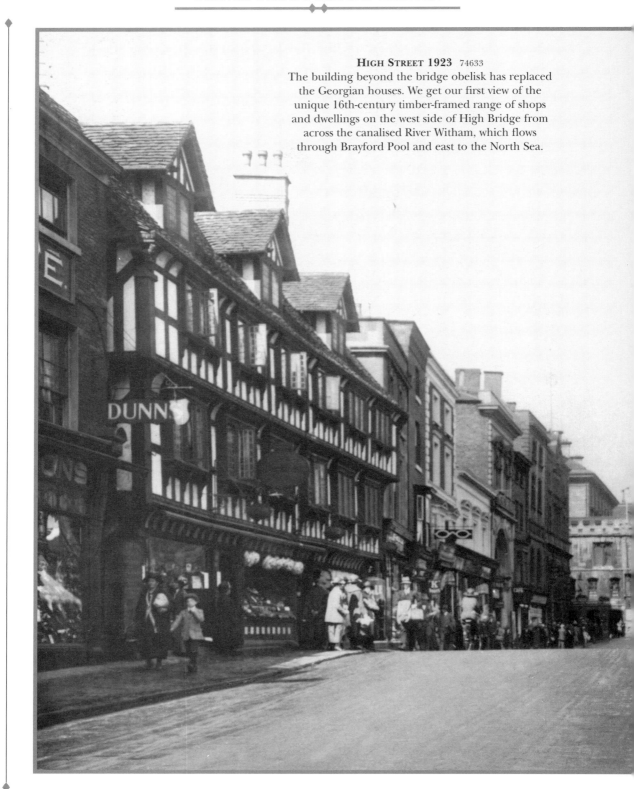

HIGH STREET 1923 74633
The building beyond the bridge obelisk has replaced
the Georgian houses. We get our first view of the
unique 16th-century timber-framed range of shops
and dwellings on the west side of High Bridge from
across the canalised River Witham, which flows
through Brayford Pool and east to the North Sea.

THE CATHEDRAL AND HIGH STREET c1950 L49041

HIGH BRIDGE 1923 74637

THE CATHEDRAL AND HIGH STREET c1950

The buildings on the left made way for Marks and Spencer in the 1930s, which was since rebuilt again in 1973. The refined Flemish Renaissance building to the right of Curry's Radio House is a scholarly piece built in 1900. Curry's, and the gabled building beyond, have been demolished, and the obelisk on the bridge went in 1939.

◆

HIGH BRIDGE 1923

Moving east into Waterside, which flanks the River Witham, look back to High Bridge. The Obelisk, erected soon after 1763, commemorates a chapel which stood on the east side of the bridge until 1762; it was dedicated to St Thomas of Canterbury, who was martyred in 1170. It seems to have been built by 1200.

HIGH BRIDGE C1950 L49036

The bridge itself is late 12th-century, but much restored, and in this view the Obelisk has gone, taken down in February 1939. The early 19th-century Café building to the left of the timber-framed bridge buildings was replaced by the 1930s heavy-handed baroque-ish Marks and Spencer with its giant pilasters linked by swags, itself demolished in 1973.

HIGH BRIDGE C1955 L49094

By this time the shabby building on the far left has been taken over by Burton's, now also demolished, while the 1907 building to the right, disfigured by an outside stairway, has also gone. This site is now the rather impressive 1990s Waterside shopping centre which has shops on three floors.

HIGH BRIDGE 1890 25659

In 1890 the timber-framed buildings on the west side of High Bridge were in a highly decayed state, as seen in this 1890 view. Picturesque but tottering, in 1900 they were partly rebuilt and restored by William Watkins. The buildings to left and right in this view have also gone.

THE GLORY HOLE 1923 74639

The area west of High Bridge was known as the Glory Hole. The buildings on the right went in the 1930s to be replaced by a Marks and Spencer, but Mumby and Sons' tall warehouse on the left survives, and has been well converted into a solicitor's offices.

THE GLORY HOLE 1906 55112

In this view we see the largely rebuilt High Bridge buildings with the brickwork and stonework still looking fresh.
In the roof William Watkins added three authentically 15th-century style dormer windows. All the cottages on the
left were demolished by 1910. Both sides of the water were reached by stairs from the High Street.

THE GLORY HOLE c1910 55112A

The replacement buildings for the cottages are in place by this time, and indeed still survive. Part of the High
Bridge building is a café to which I remember being taken as a small boy when staying with my grandparents
in Gainsborough.

THE GREEN DRAGON HOTEL c1955 L49130

THE GREEN DRAGON HOTEL c1955
Further east along Waterside, past the
Waterside shopping centre, are a pair of
fine timber-framed buildings, both
restored: the 16th-century Witch and
Wardrobe, out of view to the left, and the
Green Dragon seen here, which is close
to where Broadgate's Thorn Bridge cross-
es the Witham. The present bridge of
1940 replaces the old Magpies
Bridge of 1858.

THE GREEN DRAGON HOTEL c1955
The Green Dragon pub is a heavily
restored fourteenth-century timber-
framed building with a stone ground
floor and two jettied or projecting upper
storeys. The blank site behind is now
occupied by Thorngate House, a nasty
1960s office block: not a very attractive
backdrop to this old merchant's house.

THE GREEN DRAGON HOTEL c1955 L49117

HIGH STREET c1950 L49039
Looking south from High Bridge beside Marks and Spencer, beyond the Italianate mid-19th-century Barclays Bank (now rebuilt in glass and metal) you can see the 11th-century church tower of St Mary le Wigford. On the right is Lloyds TSB bank of 1900; its tall cupola has been demolished above the balustrades.

HIGH STREET c1950 L49016
Much further south along the High Street is St Mary's Guildhall at the junction with Sibthorp Street. This Norman building of about 1170 is a remarkable survival of a medieval trade guild's hall and chambers and is now the base of the Lincoln Civic Trust. The elaborate baroque-style tower on the left belongs to the Central Methodist Church of 1905.

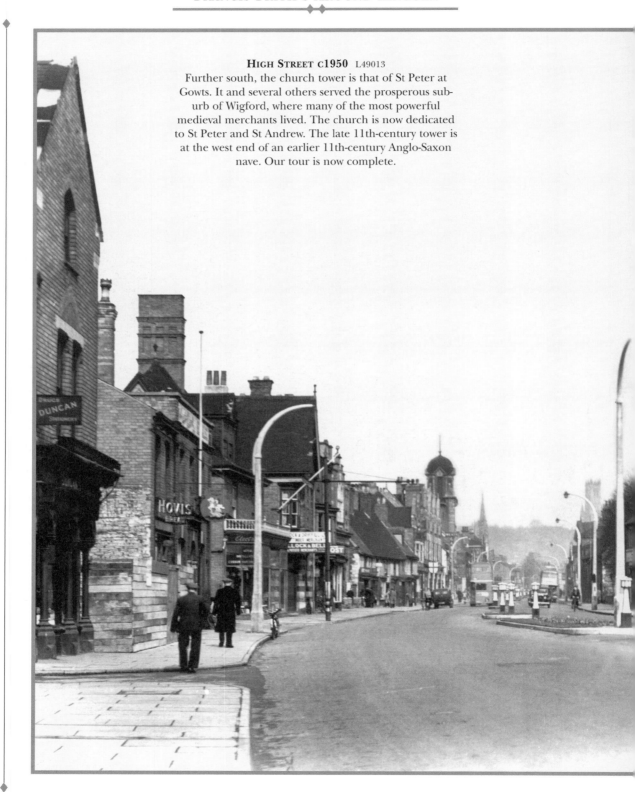

HIGH STREET c1950 L49013
Further south, the church tower is that of St Peter at
Gowts. It and several others served the prosperous sub-
urb of Wigford, where many of the most powerful
medieval merchants lived. The church is now dedicated
to St Peter and St Andrew. The late 11th-century tower is
at the west end of an earlier 11th-century Anglo-Saxon
nave. Our tour is now complete.

GAINSBOROUGH, MARKET PLACE C1955   G145009

Our tour of the towns and villages near Lincoln starts in Gainsborough, a town of the ancient Anglo-Saxon kingdom of Lindsey that ruled what is now north Lincolnshire. A medieval market town, its present Town Hall only dates from 1891, seen here before the tepid 1956 Neo-Georgian facade was added with shops to the ground floor.

GAINSBOROUGH, MARKET PLACE 1955 G145014

At a strategic crossing point of the River Trent, it is an ancient market town; its planned street layout focuses on the Market Place, whose most architecturally distinguished building is the old National Provincial Bank, now the Natwest. It is an exuberant Neo-Georgian piece of 1926 with a semi-circular portico on columns; most of its neighbours to the right have now gone.

GAINSBOROUGH, MARKET STREET c1955 G145034
This view looks along Market Street towards the Town Hall from the junction with Beaumont Street, whose east side is mostly occupied by the enormously long frontage of the former Marshall's Britannia engineering works. The gap in the middle distance was caused by Gainsborough's only World War II bomb.

GAINSBOROUGH, SILVER STREET c1955 G145008

GAINSBOROUGH, THE OLD HALL c1955 G145002

GAINSBOROUGH
Silver Street c1955

Silver Street led from the Market place to the river, which was lined by the warehouses and factories of this once busy inland port, including my grandfather's Rose Brothers, a packaging machinery works swept away along with most of the warehouses in recent years. Silver Street, now pedestrianised, retains most of its old character, however.

◆

GAINSBOROUGH
The Old Hall c1955

The centrepiece of the town is undoubtedly the great 15th-century mansion of the de Burghs, the Old Hall, set in a grassed square surrounded by Victorian housing. Here we see the great castle-like north-east corner tower and, to the right, the Great Hall's oriel bay window and the (now glazed) cupola to vent the hall's former open fire.

GAINSBOROUGH, THE OLD HALL c1955 G145001
From the south you can see the Hall's plan clearly, with the central Great Hall behind the three timber-framed gables of Hickman's 1597 stair and corridor addition. The private apartments were in the right wing, and the lodgings or guest range in the left. The Hall, now well cared for, spent centuries in decay, and was once a factory and tenements.

SAXILBY, HIGH STREET c1965 S481022
Moving south towards Lincoln we reach the large village of Saxilby. Two transport modes profoundly influenced its development: the Roman Foss Dyke canal that linked Lincoln to the River Trent, and the more recent railway which arrived in 1849. The white gate beyond the former St Andrew's Church of 1879 leads to the station off the High Street.

SAXILBY, WATERSIDE C1955 S481001

SAXILBY
Waterside c1955
Further south is the Foss Dyke. In the middle distance is the site of the old swing bridge, now replaced by the present 1937 bridge on the A57 bypass upon which the photographer is standing. The arch is that to the 1911 pipe bridge that carries Lincoln's water from Nottinghamshire. The present footbridge is a Victorian one placed here in 1987.

◆

DODDINGTON
The Village 1906
Doddington, west of Lincoln, is a delightful small village, very much focussed around its Hall, a large late Elizabethan mansion built for Thomas Taylor, Recorder to the Bishop of Lincoln. The trees in the distance on the left mark its forecourt in this tranquil view looking north. The main change nowadays is the rather necessary addition of pavements

DODDINGTON, THE VILLAGE 1906 55116

DODDINGTON, THE CHURCH 1906 55117

Doddington receives many visitors, for Doddington Hall, although privately owned, is often open to the public. Immediately north-east of the Hall is St Peter's Church, almost entirely rebuilt in the 1770s by Thomas Lumby in partly scholarly Gothic, although a cheery Strawberry Hill Gothick breaks out here and there, particularly in the west tower.

WADDINGTON, HIGH STREET c1960 W2006

Waddington is now noted more for its large Royal Air Force station to the east of the village, but it grew up on a diversion of Ermine Street to the western scarp of the limestone ridge. Consequently much of the village is built of the local oolitic limestone, which gives it a coherent character. This view looks north along the High Street.

WADDINGTON, HIGH STREET c1960 W2011

The village lost its medieval church to bombs in World War II and has expanded much since the War, partly due to Lincoln's proximity and partly to the RAF. In this view we look past the Horse and Jockey pub towards the south of the village; the church is beyond the high tree on the left.

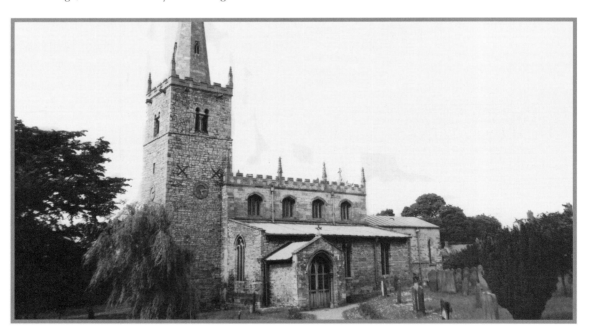

BRANSTON, THE CHURCH c1955 B512001

Further east, Branston concludes this brief tour. It is a charming village with winding lanes centring on its partly Anglo-Saxon All Saints church. It has distinctive 'long and short work' quoins to the west end of the nave; the 11th-century tower is Saxon but with Norman west doorway and arcading, and the neat spire is 15th-century.

Index

Frith Book Co Titles

www.francisfrith.co.uk

The Frith Book Company publishes over 100 new titles each year. A selection of those currently available are listed below. For latest catalogue please contact Frith Book Co.

Town Books 96pages, approx 100 photos. County and Themed Books 128pages, approx 150 photos (unless specified). All titles hardback laminated case and jacket except those indicated pb (paperback)

Title	ISBN	Price	Title	ISBN	Price
Amersham, Chesham & Rickmansworth (pb)	1-85937-340-2	£9.99	Derby (pb)	1-85937-367-4	£9.99
Ancient Monuments & Stone Circles	1-85937-143-4	£17.99	Derbyshire (pb)	1-85937-196-5	£9.99
Aylesbury (pb)	1-85937-227-9	£9.99	Devon (pb)	1-85937-297-x	£9.99
Bakewell	1-85937-113-2	£12.99	Dorset (pb)	1-85937-269-4	£9.99
Barnstaple (pb)	1-85937-300-3	£9.99	Dorset Churches	1-85937-172-8	£17.99
Bath (pb)	1-85937419-0	£9.99	Dorset Coast (pb)	1-85937-299-6	£9.99
Bedford (pb)	1-85937-205-8	£9.99	Dorset Living Memories	1-85937-210-4	£14.99
Berkshire (pb)	1-85937-191-4	£9.99	Down the Severn	1-85937-118-3	£14.99
Berkshire Churches	1-85937-170-1	£17.99	Down the Thames (pb)	1-85937-278-3	£9.99
Blackpool (pb)	1-85937-382-8	£9.99	Down the Trent	1-85937-311-9	£14.99
Bognor Regis (pb)	1-85937-431-x	£9.99	Dublin (pb)	1-85937-231-7	£9.99
Bournemouth	1-85937-067-5	£12.99	East Anglia (pb)	1-85937-265-1	£9.99
Bradford (pb)	1-85937-204-x	£9.99	East London	1-85937-080-2	£14.99
Brighton & Hove(pb)	1-85937-192-2	£8.99	East Sussex	1-85937-130-2	£14.99
Bristol (pb)	1-85937-264-3	£9.99	Eastbourne	1-85937-061-6	£12.99
British Life A Century Ago (pb)	1-85937-213-9	£9.99	Edinburgh (pb)	1-85937-193-0	£8.99
Buckinghamshire (pb)	1-85937-200-7	£9.99	England in the 1880s	1-85937-331-3	£17.99
Camberley (pb)	1-85937-222-8	£9.99	English Castles (pb)	1-85937-434-4	£9.99
Cambridge (pb)	1-85937-422-0	£9.99	English Country Houses	1-85937-161-2	£17.99
Cambridgeshire (pb)	1-85937-420-4	£9.99	Essex (pb)	1-85937-270-8	£9.99
Canals & Waterways (pb)	1-85937-291-0	£9.99	Exeter	1-85937-126-4	£12.99
Canterbury Cathedral (pb)	1-85937-179-5	£9.99	Exmoor	1-85937-132-9	£14.99
Cardiff (pb)	1-85937-093-4	£9.99	Falmouth	1-85937-066-7	£12.99
Carmarthenshire	1-85937-216-3	£14.99	Folkestone (pb)	1-85937-124-8	£9.99
Chelmsford (pb)	1-85937-310-0	£9.99	Glasgow (pb)	1-85937-190-6	£9.99
Cheltenham (pb)	1-85937-095-0	£9.99	Gloucestershire	1-85937-102-7	£14.99
Cheshire (pb)	1-85937-271-6	£9.99	Great Yarmouth (pb)	1-85937-426-3	£9.99
Chester	1-85937-090-x	£12.99	Greater Manchester (pb)	1-85937-266-x	£9.99
Chesterfield	1-85937-378-x	£9.99	Guildford (pb)	1-85937-410-7	£9.99
Chichester (pb)	1-85937-228-7	£9.99	Hampshire (pb)	1-85937-279-1	£9.99
Colchester (pb)	1-85937-188-4	£8.99	Hampshire Churches (pb)	1-85937-207-4	£9.99
Cornish Coast	1-85937-163-9	£14.99	Harrogate	1-85937-423-9	£9.99
Cornwall (pb)	1-85937-229-5	£9.99	Hastings & Bexhill (pb)	1-85937-131-0	£9.99
Cornwall Living Memories	1-85937-248-1	£14.99	Heart of Lancashire (pb)	1-85937-197-3	£9.99
Cotswolds (pb)	1-85937-230-9	£9.99	Helston (pb)	1-85937-214-7	£9.99
Cotswolds Living Memories	1-85937-255-4	£14.99	Hereford (pb)	1-85937-175-2	£9.99
County Durham	1-85937-123-x	£14.99	Herefordshire	1-85937-174-4	£14.99
Croydon Living Memories	1-85937-162-0	£9.99	Hertfordshire (pb)	1-85937-247-3	£9.99
Cumbria	1-85937-101-9	£14.99	Horsham (pb)	1-85937-432-8	£9.99
Dartmoor	1-85937-145-0	£14.99	Humberside	1-85937-215-5	£14.99
			Hythe, Romney Marsh & Ashford	1-85937-256-2	£9.99

Available from your local bookshop or from the publisher

Frith Book Co Titles (continued)

Title	ISBN	Price	Title	ISBN	Price
Ipswich (pb)	1-85937-424-7	£9.99	St Ives (pb)	1-85937415-8	£9.99
Ireland (pb)	1-85937-181-7	£9.99	Scotland (pb)	1-85937-182-5	£9.99
Isle of Man (pb)	1-85937-268-6	£9.99	Scottish Castles (pb)	1-85937-323-2	£9.99
Isles of Scilly	1-85937-136-1	£14.99	Sevenoaks & Tunbridge	1-85937-057-8	£12.99
Isle of Wight (pb)	1-85937-429-8	£9.99	Sheffield, South Yorks (pb)	1-85937-267-8	£9.99
Isle of Wight Living Memories	1-85937-304-6	£14.99	Shrewsbury (pb)	1-85937-325-9	£9.99
Kent (pb)	1-85937-189-2	£9.99	Shropshire (pb)	1-85937-326-7	£9.99
Kent Living Memories	1-85937-125-6	£14.99	Somerset	1-85937-153-1	£14.99
Lake District (pb)	1-85937-275-9	£9.99	South Devon Coast	1-85937-107-8	£14.99
Lancaster, Morecambe & Heysham (pb)	1-85937-233-3	£9.99	South Devon Living Memories	1-85937-168-x	£14.99
Leeds (pb)	1-85937-202-3	£9.99	South Hams	1-85937-220-1	£14.99
Leicester	1-85937-073-x	£12.99	Southampton (pb)	1-85937-427-1	£9.99
Leicestershire (pb)	1-85937-185-x	£9.99	Southport (pb)	1-85937-425-5	£9.99
Lincolnshire (pb)	1-85937-433-6	£9.99	Staffordshire	1-85937-047-0	£12.99
Liverpool & Merseyside (pb)	1-85937-234-1	£9.99	Stratford upon Avon	1-85937-098-5	£12.99
London (pb)	1-85937-183-3	£9.99	Suffolk (pb)	1-85937-221-x	£9.99
Ludlow (pb)	1-85937-176-0	£9.99	Suffolk Coast	1-85937-259-7	£14.99
Luton (pb)	1-85937-235-x	£9.99	Surrey (pb)	1-85937-240-6	£9.99
Maidstone	1-85937-056-x	£14.99	Sussex (pb)	1-85937-184-1	£9.99
Manchester (pb)	1-85937-198-1	£9.99	Swansea (pb)	1-85937-167-1	£9.99
Middlesex	1-85937-158-2	£14.99	Tees Valley & Cleveland	1-85937-211-2	£14.99
New Forest	1-85937-128-0	£14.99	Thanet (pb)	1-85937-116-7	£9.99
Newark (pb)	1-85937-366-6	£9.99	Tiverton (pb)	1-85937-178-7	£9.99
Newport, Wales (pb)	1-85937-258-9	£9.99	Torbay	1-85937-063-2	£12.99
Newquay (pb)	1-85937-421-2	£9.99	Truro	1-85937-147-7	£12.99
Norfolk (pb)	1-85937-195-7	£9.99	Victorian and Edwardian Cornwall	1-85937-252-x	£14.99
Norfolk Living Memories	1-85937-217-1	£14.99	Victorian & Edwardian Devon	1-85937-253-8	£14.99
Northamptonshire	1-85937-150-7	£14.99	Victorian & Edwardian Kent	1-85937-149-3	£14.99
Northumberland Tyne & Wear (pb)	1-85937-281-3	£9.99	Vic & Ed Maritime Album	1-85937-144-2	£17.99
North Devon Coast	1-85937-146-9	£14.99	Victorian and Edwardian Sussex	1-85937-157-4	£14.99
North Devon Living Memories	1-85937-261-9	£14.99	Victorian & Edwardian Yorkshire	1-85937-154-x	£14.99
North London	1-85937-206-6	£14.99	Victorian Seaside	1-85937-159-0	£17.99
North Wales (pb)	1-85937-298-8	£9.99	Villages of Devon (pb)	1-85937-293-7	£9.99
North Yorkshire (pb)	1-85937-236-8	£9.99	Villages of Kent (pb)	1-85937-294-5	£9.99
Norwich (pb)	1-85937-194-9	£8.99	Villages of Sussex (pb)	1-85937-295-3	£9.99
Nottingham (pb)	1-85937-324-0	£9.99	Warwickshire (pb)	1-85937-203-1	£9.99
Nottinghamshire (pb)	1-85937-187-6	£9.99	Welsh Castles (pb)	1-85937-322-4	£9.99
Oxford (pb)	1-85937-411-5	£9.99	West Midlands (pb)	1-85937-289-9	£9.99
Oxfordshire (pb)	1-85937-430-1	£9.99	West Sussex	1-85937-148-5	£14.99
Peak District (pb)	1-85937-280-5	£9.99	West Yorkshire (pb)	1-85937-201-5	£9.99
Penzance	1-85937-069-1	£12.99	Weymouth (pb)	1-85937-209-0	£9.99
Peterborough (pb)	1-85937-219-8	£9.99	Wiltshire (pb)	1-85937-277-5	£9.99
Piers	1-85937-237-6	£17.99	Wiltshire Churches (pb)	1-85937-171-x	£9.99
Plymouth	1-85937-119-1	£12.99	Wiltshire Living Memories	1-85937-245-7	£14.99
Poole & Sandbanks (pb)	1-85937-251-1	£9.99	Winchester (pb)	1-85937-428-x	£9.99
Preston (pb)	1-85937-212-0	£9.99	Windmills & Watermills	1-85937-242-2	£17.99
Reading (pb)	1-85937-238-4	£9.99	Worcester (pb)	1-85937-165-5	£9.99
Romford (pb)	1-85937-319-4	£9.99	Worcestershire	1-85937-152-3	£14.99
Salisbury (pb)	1-85937-239-2	£9.99	York (pb)	1-85937-199-x	£9.99
Scarborough (pb)	1-85937-379-8	£9.99	Yorkshire (pb)	1-85937-186-8	£9.99
St Albans (pb)	1-85937-341-0	£9.99	Yorkshire Living Memories	1-85937-166-3	£14.99

See Frith books on the internet www.francisfrith.co.uk

FRITH PRODUCTS & SERVICES

Francis Frith would doubtless be pleased to know that the pioneering publishing venture he started in 1860 still continues today. A hundred and forty years later, The Francis Frith Collection continues in the same innovative tradition and is now one of the foremost publishers of vintage photographs in the world. Some of the current activities include:

Interior Decoration

Today Frith's photographs can be seen framed and as giant wall murals in thousands of pubs, restaurants, hotels, banks, retail stores and other public buildings throughout the country. In every case they enhance the unique local atmosphere of the places they depict and provide reminders of gentler days in an increasingly busy and frenetic world.

Product Promotions

Frith products are used by many major companies to promote the sales of their own products or to reinforce their own history and heritage. Frith promotions have been used by Hovis bread, Courage beers, Scots Porage Oats, Colman's mustard, Cadbury's foods, Mellow Birds coffee, Dunhill pipe tobacco, Guinness, and Bulmer's Cider.

Genealogy and Family History

As the interest in family history and roots grows world-wide, more and more people are turning to Frith's photographs of Great Britain for images of the towns, villages and streets where their ancestors lived; and, of course, photographs of the churches and chapels where their ancestors were christened, married and buried are an essential part of every genealogy tree and family album.

Frith Products

All Frith photographs are available Framed or just as Mounted Prints and Posters (size 23 x 16 inches). These may be ordered from the address below. From time to time other products - Address Books, Calendars, Table Mats, etc - are available.

The Internet

Already twenty thousand Frith photographs can be viewed and purchased on the internet through the Frith websites and a myriad of partner sites.

For more detailed information on Frith companies and products, look at these sites:

www.francisfrith.co.uk
www.francisfrith.com
(for North American visitors)

See the complete list of Frith Books at:

www.francisfrith.co.uk

This web site is regularly updated with the latest list of publications from the Frith Book Company. If you wish to buy books relating to another part of the country that your local bookshop does not stock, you may purchase on-line.

For further information, trade, or author enquiries please contact us at the address below:
The Francis Frith Collection, Frith's Barn, Teffont, Salisbury, Wiltshire, England SP3 5QP.
Tel: +44 (0)1722 716 376 Fax: +44 (0)1722 716 881   Email: sales@francisfrith.co.uk

---

See Frith books on the internet www.francisfrith.co.uk